Pepper's adventure

Story by Beverley Randell

Illustrated by Priscilla Cutter

One day Dad came home
with two pet mice
in a little cage.
Sarah loved them.
She called the brown one Pepper
and the white one Salt.

Dad made a big new cage
for Pepper and Salt.
It had a wheel and a ladder
and a room upstairs.
Sarah played with the mice a lot,
and so did Nicky from next door.
"Don't take them outside,"
said Mom.

But one day Nicky **did** take
Pepper outside.
"No! Don't do that!" said Sarah.
"Bring Pepper back inside!"

But Nicky put Pepper
down on the grass
to see if he liked it, and . . .

8

. . . Pepper ran away!

He ran into a flower bed.

"I'm sorry!" said Nicky.

Nicky **was** sorry,
but that did not
bring Pepper back.

Pepper had gone.

9

There are lots of hiding places
in a garden
for a little brown mouse.
The children looked for Pepper
but they did not find him.
"A cat may get him
and eat him up!" said Sarah.
Nicky went home crying.

"Let's put Pepper's little cage out in the garden," said Mom. "Maybe he will **want** to go back inside his old home."

Sarah put some food in the cage. "Pepper will be hungry," she said.

Mom and Sarah put the cage down
in the flowers. They opened
the door, but Pepper did not come.

They had to go back to the house
without him.
Sarah went to tell Salt.
"Pepper has gone," she said. But . . .

. . . at bedtime they looked again, and there, sitting inside his old cage, was Pepper!

"Salt will be pleased," said Sarah – and Salt **was**.

16